CHILDREN'S SERMONS
for the Revised Common Lectionary
Year A

CHILDREN'S SERMONS
for the Revised Common Lectionary
Year A
Using the 5 Senses to Tell God's Story

PHILIP D. SCHROEDER

ABINGDON PRESS
Nashville

Children's Sermons for the Revised Common Lectionary
Year A
Copyright © 1997 by Abingdon Press

Scripture quotations, unless otherwise noted, are from the New Revised Standard Version Bible, Copyright © 1989, by the Division of Christian Education of the National Council of the Churches of Christ in the USA. Used by permission.

This book is printed on recycled, acid-free paper.

Book design by J. S. Lofbomm

Schroeder, Philip D., 1964-
    Children's sermons for the revised common lectionary : using the 5 senses to tell God's story / Philip D. Schroeder.
        p. cm.
    Contents: [1]. Year A—[2]. Year B—[3]. Year C.
    ISBN 0-687-04996-2 (pbk. : v. 1 : alk. paper). —ISBN 0-687-01827-7 (pbk. : v. 2 : alk. paper). —ISBN 0-687-05577-6 (pbk. : v. 3 : alk. paper)
    1. Children's sermons. 2. Preaching to children. 3. Common lectionary (1992) 4. Lectionary preaching. I. Title.
    BV4315.S335 1997
    251 ' . 53—dc21   97-14948
                                                                                    CIP

02 03 04 05 06—10 9 8 7 6 5 4

*For our children
Daniel, Kathryn, and Paul*

CONTENTS

Extension agents in Georgia often relate this story about the possibilities for children to act as catalysts for change. It seems that the newly appointed cooperative extension agent was struggling to convince the local farmers to use all the new and innovative farming methods being touted by the University of Georgia. He knew that such methods and ideas would increase the size and quality of vegetable production for these farmers. The agent went from farm to farm trying to convince any farmer who would listen of the advantages of his "newfangled" ways of planting and fertilizing, but the farmers wouldn't hear of it. They weren't going to have an outsider come into their county and tell them that their granddaddy's way of planting corn wasn't good enough anymore. Like that old-time religion, that old-time agriculture was good enough for them.

Then the extension agent came up with a brilliant idea. Why not hold a contest for the children of the community to see who could grow the best produce? A Corn Club was begun for boys as they tried to grow the biggest ears of corn. A Tomato Club was started for the girls who grew, harvested, and canned the most tomatoes from their family's gardens. The competition had implications beyond winners and losers. Increased corn production meant more money for the family and more grain to feed the farm animals. Canned tomatoes provided many meals for families who had to grow their own food. Miraculously, many of the children began to reap more bountiful harvests than their parents, the farmers. Through their children, the parents were indirectly invited into learning the new processes and were not threatened by the new ideas, for these were "just kids." Soon the adults began to ask how they, too, could grow such beautiful produce, and in stepped the same cooperative extension agent to share these "newfangled" methods with the eager farmers, who had been transformed by the seeds their children and the county extension agent had planted. What started in 1917 as Corn and Tomato Clubs are known as 4-H Clubs today.

Using children as the catalyst for change is not a new idea. Jesus himself pulled a child from the crowd to make a point in his own process for stimulating renewal. His methods featured parables that shattered preconceptions and left his listeners holding the paradox! Applying this concept of children acting as agents of change to the worship setting can provide an avenue for congregational transformation. Children hold promise and can lead the way through the sands shifting beneath our feet and into the new paradigms emerging in front of our eyes, ears, mouths, hands, and noses. Too often children are seen as agents of destruction because they seemingly disturb the solemnity of the sanctuary, but their very presence often sets a community of faith in motion.

Significant and meaningful change within the church can take place only if we recognize the importance of tradition. Items of value are not destroyed or replaced, but are disassembled, reorganized, and then rebuilt into a new creation by the God who makes all things new using the same building blocks. Children, the most recently created, can help us in the learning process of rebuilding for the future.

In a recent interview, Bill Gates, the mind behind Microsoft, commented that children are not necessarily more proficient than adults, but rather more willing to learn. He said that adults for the most part are unwilling to put up with the several hours of confusion necessary to learn basic computer skills. Children, on the other hand, are in a learning curve all the time and are often "confused" at the proliferation of data. They abide momentary darkness in hope of light better than adults.[1]

An Objection to the Object Lesson

Worship is a mystery, not a collection of skills to master or a body of knowledge to be understood. It is an experience to be lived. We learn to worship by worshiping! Children learn to worship by collecting experiences of worship.[2]

The majority of modern homiletical techniques focus on the two-dimensional illustration, the word picture, as the customary approach to the preaching task. The preacher seeks to illuminate a text with examples, stories, and analogies that help the listener hear and understand the message of the text in contemporary terms. To illustrate literally means to light up. Light allows the object to be examined more closely, but it remains an object. The *object lesson,* the most common method for sharing the gospel with children, asks children not only to make cognitive metaphorical connections that are beyond their grasp, but also to remain objective, never becoming subjects of the gospel.

> *TRY THIS EXPERIMENT: Assemble a group of children in a room. Place a painting on one side of the room; on the other side, place a television playing a children's video. Where will the children gravitate? Your experiment will probably show that the shift from the still life picture to the moving picture has already occurred in the lives of your children.*

The children's sermon seems trapped in the age of the still life illustration or object lesson, the product of an earlier era. William Armstrong, author of the late-nineteenth-century book entitled *Five Minute Sermons to Children,* also struggled to find the most appropriate way to share the gospel with children. He understood that preaching to children took preparation but soon discovered that thirty minutes was too long for children's time! He finally settled on a five-minute children's sermon period that took into consideration his audience's attention span. His methodology is briefly summarized in the final words of his preface:

> Illustration is a necessity in all preaching (witness that of Christ), but especially in preaching to children. We all love pictures, but children love them most, and an illustration is a word-picture. An object sermon, if short and pointed, has a fine effect.[3]

Although Jesus did paint word pictures, it appears that he used far more than just object lessons to bring the gospel to life. Jesus was a multisensory teacher. He taught in ways that stimulated all the senses. Tasting, hearing, touching, seeing, and smelling were all part of his ministry.

Jesus helped those around him to taste and see that the Lord is good. He ate with sinners and tax collectors. He kept a party going by transforming water into wine. He taught the disciples by gathering grain to eat on the Sabbath. He broke bread and shared wine with his disciples who literally tasted the good news. Even after the Resurrection, Jesus asked for something to eat.

Jesus proclaimed the kingdom of God with his voice, and the people heard in new ways. He taught in parables that encouraged the hearers to listen, to reflect, and to respond. He invited people into the frames of his stories to struggle with the challenge of his words.

Jesus was constantly touching people while others struggled to touch him. When Jesus touched people to heal them, those around him claimed that in that touching, he taught with authority.

Jesus gave sight to people who had no sight and insight to the sighted. He pointed out scenes in their lives such as the widow's mite and told them to look at a coin to see whose picture was on it. He reminded them, "Blessed are the poor in spirit, for theirs is the kingdom of heaven."

Jesus was anointed for burial by Mary, Lazarus and Martha's sister. As the smell of that perfume drifted through the air, he taught of his impending death. (Jesus never seems to heal anyone who could not smell, but I suspect the lack of an olfactory capacity was a blessing in those days.)

Jesus used all the senses to communicate his message.

Swiss psychologist Jean Piaget argued that children actively construct reality out of their experiences with the environment rather than mimick what they encounter. Children live and learn rather than learn to live in the environment that is already in place. Everything does not have to be explained as it occurs, but as the child develops, she will begin to categorize and theologize about her experiences and draw her own conclusions.

In the first approximately two years of life, the sensorimotor period, children perceive only the existence of things that are within the immediate grasp of their senses. If they cannot taste, hear, touch, see, or smell something, it no longer exists in their world construct. This childhood stage features a sense of connectedness to all things. The child does not have a sense of where her body stops and everything else begins.[4]

This stage informs our human difficulty with affirming a God we cannot know through our senses. If an infant believes only in what she can sense, then are we not all infants in many ways? Children learn in this stage not by impersonal abstractions or arm's length study, but by an active physical interaction with the animate persons and inanimate objects in their lives. This stage is a time of exploring the world around them. Therefore, the children's sermon can be another opportunity for such exploration. It can be a safe time to learn to trust their environment and those around them. Children's sermons can respond to a child's search for things that are trustworthy in life. This first stage of learning, the lowest common denominator shared by all of humanity, can be the starting point for the children's sermon. If the children's sermon appeals to sensorimotor experiences, it will connect with all people on some level.

Object lessons may stimulate the senses of seeing, hearing, and touching, but there is little interaction with the object. At a church I recently visited, I listened as the minister showed the children a picture of an elephant. He asked the children, "How many of you have acted like elephants this week?" Blank stares were the response. A sensorimotor children's sermon on the same subject might have given each child the chance to behave like an elephant and discuss that behavior rather than merely talk about how elephants act. Object lessons allow people to remain objective, maintaining an "I-It" relationship; but Jesus set people in motion toward "I-Thou" relationships with God and one another. Jesus began a movement, yet many persons have sought to make him the object of their worship, an icon to be worshiped on the desktop of life. The life of Jesus is then used to illustrate a point instead of allowing his presence to be experienced in our daily lives. Christianity is not a still life picture, but a moving, spirited faith.

The Alternative—The Multisensory Subject Lesson

Multimedia can be defined as the confluence of written text, graphics such as photos, videos, illustrations, animation, and sound, such as speech and music to achieve a multisensory stimulation. Many multimedia computer programs have been labeled as "edutainment" products as the boundaries between learning and play have begun to blur. Computers allow for interactive learning when new lessons are constantly reinforced through the use of multiple senses at once.

Retention levels for all types of learning increase drastically when more than one sense is used to transmit the message.

TRY THIS EXERCISE: Make a list of all the scripture passages you have memorized. Now make a list of all the hymns you know by heart. Which list is longer?

When words and melodies are combined, our minds retain more information. Multisensory children's sermons can help children to recall more of what has been presented, even though conveying factual knowledge is not the sole purpose of the children's sermon. Contrary to popular belief, entertainment for the children or the adults is not the goal of the children's sermon. Interestingly enough, entertainment has long been associated with passivity on the part of the one being entertained, but now entertainment is more participative than ever as people search for primary experiences. Children's sermons are more about experiencing the gospel for transformation and formation rather than for information or entertainment. Children learn by doing.

Children's sermons can be designed to develop relationships, establishing a level of trust between the leaders and the children while helping youngsters discover God in their own lives by hearing and participating in the retelling of the stories of God's people.

The same phenomenon seems to have found its way into many of our mainline Protestant churches as a congregation of spectators watch one person regulating the interaction. The sermon takes the form of a lecture, and the people are expected to consume the product being presented without response. In the silent print medium, there is no way of knowing whether or not you have, in fact, communicated your point when a person reads a document that you have written. Critiques and reviews of your presentation only continue the muted volleying between monologues. The shift in homiletics toward including an experience moves the people in the pews from observers to participants. By surrendering interpretive control of the presented experience, the sensorimotor children's sermon experience invites interaction between the worship leader, the children, and the entire congregation.

TRY ANOTHER EXPERIMENT: This time, instead of two choices, add a third dimension. Place a painting on one side of the room, a television with a VCR playing a video on another side of the room, and a multimedia computer displaying the most recently released Living Book CD-ROM in another spot. To which side will the children gravitate? A few children will still turn to the television to be entertained. Others will be fascinated with their ability to interact with the CD-ROM program, but only one child will ultimately be able to do so. Children sitting on the sidelines observing the multimedia presentation may soon opt for the television, since only one person can regulate the computer interaction.

If we trace the evolution of the video game, the shift in the perspective of the player in relationship to the game suggests this contemporary movement from observer to participant. The first video game, PONG, allowed the player to manipulate objects on a screen in order to prevent a small ball of light from moving off the edge of the screen. The ball never came toward the player, but remained an object that merely floated back and forth across the screen. As technology improved, games such as Space Invaders gave the player the visual and auditory feeling that aliens were getting closer to the bottom of the screen, which is where the player's hands reside, but still the "I-It" relationship remained. Then innovative games began to feature characters that looked out of the screen toward the player. Actions were performed with the movement of a simple joystick and the pressing of various buttons.

Currently, video games have changed their perspective so the player is not merely a manipulator of pieces disconnected to his or her physical space. The player becomes one of the characters in the story. Racing games no longer feature tiny cars that move around a circular track fully displayed in front of the driver. The driver is invited to sit behind the wheel and drive down a road that opens up directly in front of him or her. The player not only moves the car, but the car is designed so as to make the driver feel the bumps in the road by shaking the steering wheel upon impact. This change in perspective moves the player from the position of an interested observer to an actual subject within the game.

Virtual reality invites us to a place where we become a part of the movement, a place where we can discover things for ourselves. Virtual reality, the experience of perceiving and interacting through sensors and effectors with a computer-modeled environment, is essentially about world building. Virtual reality creates places where drug researchers can assemble virtual molecules, where doctors can practice surgical skills on computer-generated patients, where astronauts can simulate Mars landings, and where architects can walk through dream homes. While many of these applications seem futuristic, virtual reality is already routinely used in airline flight simulators enabling pilots to hone their abilities to handle increasingly complex modern aircraft. Virtual reality provides a place for us to explore, to gain knowledge, and to practice skills we have acquired. With the advent of the multisensory experiences of multimedia and virtual reality, the dominant method of communication has shifted from the silently read, written word to the echoing and reverberating moving word.

During a recent visit to a virtual reality playground featuring an interactive exploration adventure, I found the most interesting aspect of the experience was not the game itself, but the manner in which potential players were taught the game. Recruits were herded into a room with a huge video screen where they watched an eight-minute movie. The movie portrayed other rookies participating in a real-life mission similar to our virtual one. Guidance was given only through this video parable of what happened to others in similar circumstances. The recruits were invited to become part of a continuing story by stepping into this virtual world.

Virtual reality in its current state has some severe limitations for use in the communication of the biblical text. As our earlier experiment illustrates, virtual reality often lacks a communal aspect and approaches the same individualism associated with the silently read text. I propose that the church embrace a *vital ritual reality* that takes the participatory stance of virtual reality and includes the virtues of the communal experience. As the community of faith gathers to share in the Eucharist, where the inanimate becomes animate, the story of our faith is not only retold, but also relived.

Vital ritual reality gives us the opportunity to relive the story with all our senses as we taste the wine, smell the bread, touch the hands of others, hear the words of forgiveness and consecration, and see the lifted cup and broken bread.

Our children and our churches need a *vital ritual reality* in which we can feel the power of the story of Christ with all our senses and thus celebrate a dynamic faith together.

Discovering and Designing Multisensory Interactive Children's Sermons

In the new system, the audio and the visual materials are not aids; they blend with the subject matter itself to evoke an experience.[5]

18

Take a deep breath and read the following passage aloud from beginning to end without stopping to catch your breath:

> For this reason I bow my knees before the Father, from whom every family in heaven and on earth takes its name. I pray that, according to the riches of his glory, he may grant that you may be strengthened in your inner being with power through his Spirit, and that Christ may dwell in your hearts through faith, as you are being rooted and grounded in love. I pray that you may have the power to comprehend, with all the saints, what is the breadth and length and height and depth, and to know the love of Christ that surpasses knowledge, so that you may be filled with all the fullness of God. Now to him who by the power at work within us is able to accomplish abundantly far more than all we can ask or imagine, to him be glory in the church and in Christ Jesus to all generations, forever and ever. Amen. (Eph. 3:14-21)

Reading this passage without pause communicates the connectedness of the text indirectly. Rather than declaring that, in their original form, these words of the Pauline Epistle were originally written as one long sentence, you, the reader, were asked to participate in one method of experiencing a text. This method transports the words off the written page into your mouth and into your mind. Multimedia presentations advertise the possibilities for a movement from the reading of a dry text to the reception of "an earful, an eyeful, and a mind full" of the ideas being communicated by the text. By your reading aloud, your relationship with the text has changed from observer of the silent print medium to participant in the continued life of the text.

Stage One: A Preparatory Posture

A close friend, Ginger Reedy, was attempting to make her home safe for her second child who was learning to walk. With her first child, Ginger had walked around the house picking up things and moving them to the next higher level so they wouldn't be dangerous for their older child, Sarah Linn, as she took her first steps. Unfortunately, Sarah Linn found innumerable items to explore and explode, in spite of her mother's best efforts. With this information from her history, Ginger took a new posture in preparing for her second child's adventure into walking. She got down on her knees, not to pray for the strength to deal with the child, but to inspect the house from a child's point of view. Ginger discovered that there were many things to be moved that she would never have thought of from her previous angle of vision.

The starting point for the preparation of the children's sermon is also a new posture, a preparatory posture. You might begin by performing a child's view accessibility audit of your sanctuary. Walk around the sanctuary on your knees to see what you discover from a child's perspective. I have yet to see a church with a children's pew where children can sit with their feet touching the floor. (Chairs from the children's Sunday school class would provide a temporary solution in some settings.)

Children are quite literally overlooked in many sanctuaries, and we do very little to dispel the notion that this is an "adults only" space. God chose to become like us physically in order to communicate God's love to us and save us. I propose this same physical incarnational approach to our sermons with children. Unless you turn and become like a child, not only will you miss the kingdom of God, but it will also be impossible for you to really connect with children.

Preparation for children's sermons is active, not merely intellectual. Children are noisy, messy, full of energy, and occasionally disruptive. Children enjoy moving, playing, and celebrating! They tumble in the grass, run down hills at full speed, do somersaults, and spin around in circles for no other reason than the physical activity and the release of energy.

Remembering the feeling of walking along a railroad track or a curb is not the same as going out and taking that walk again. We miss certain nuances if we rely solely on our memories of our childhood rather than take the time to participate in a childhood activity. Taking a preparatory posture brings us physically into a child's world. The preparatory posture re-members us into the community of children and helps us practice for the experiences to be shared with children in worship. Just as virtual reality provides practice for real-life situations, a *vital ritual reality* invites children and adults to practice their faith. Practice helps us move easily into actual situations and gives us tools to predict when something might go wrong. Practice is itself an experience that prepares us for other experiences. We practice our sermons for the adults—at least we are supposed to—but we don't seem to practice for our time with the children even when we do take the time to prepare.

We have applied the preparatory posture to the overall creation of children's sermons, but the children's sermon most often begins with the text. The Gospel lesson from the First Sunday of Advent of Year B of the Revised Common Lectionary is Mark 13:24-37.

What type of physical posture or movement emerges from this text?

But in those days, after that suffering,
   the sun will be darkened,
      and the moon will not give its light,
   and the stars will be falling from heaven,
      and the powers in the heavens will be shaken.

Then they will see 'the Son of Man coming in clouds' with great power and glory. Then he will send out the angels, and gather his elect from the four winds, from the ends of the earth to the ends of heaven.

From the fig tree learn its lesson: as soon as its branch becomes tender and puts forth its leaves, you know that summer is near. So also, when you see these things taking place, you know that he is near, at the very gates. Truly I tell you, this generation will not pass away until all these things have taken place. Heaven and earth will pass away, but my words will not pass away.

But about that day or hour no one knows, neither the angels in heaven, nor the Son, but only the Father. Beware, keep alert; for you do not know when the time will come. It is like a man going on a journey, when he leaves home and puts his slaves in charge, each with his work, and commands the doorkeeper to be on the watch. Therefore, keep awake—for you do not know when the master of the house will come, in the evening, or at midnight, or at cockcrow, or at dawn, or else he may find you asleep when he comes suddenly. And what I say to you I say to all: Keep awake.

(Mark 13:24-37)

Possible Postures:
- Alertness, like a baseball player who keeps on his toes waiting for a ground ball or a child waiting for a parent to come home
- Asleep, curled up for a long nap
- Traveling, going on a trip, or a hike
- Yawning

The task of the preparatory posture is to encourage the sermon preparer to engage the text not only intellectually but also physically. The preparatory posture is a playful exercise. Too often we ask the children to think about waiting for Christmas or to recall trying to stay awake on Christmas Eve instead of actually creating the tension of waiting with the children as they gather. After a posture is identified, the leader is encouraged to take that stance during his or her time of preparation. Assuming a preparatory posture may mean taking a short hike, yawning a big yawn, or standing on your tiptoes. Doing this will probably feel silly at first, but it can be a valuable exercise. We communicate with children not only through our words, but also through body positions and body language. Children sense when we are uncomfortable with their postures. The preparatory posture becomes a plank from which to jump back into the text and begin the second stage of discovery.

Stage Two: The Experience

The question asked when designing the object lesson message is, "What object can I use to help me communicate a point based on the text to the children?" This method often falls prey to the "grab and stab" method of preparation as the worship leader searches the church in the minutes prior to the worship service trying to find a suitable object about which to make a point. Unfortunately, children will seldom retain the point that is trying to be forced upon them and will draw instead their own conclusions about the object in question.

If the intent of worship is to praise and experience God, the second stage poses the question, "How can I create an occasion during which the children can experience the story of God as set forth in the text?" We cannot give or teach faith to our children; we can only share the faith story as it has become our story and encourage the gift that is faith. The faith story is passed on by sharing, experiencing, and living the story together. Children and adults will grow in faith through shared experience and shared reflection.

While I was serving as an associate pastor to a church in Georgia, the senior minister was preparing to preach on "the pearl of great price." He asked me to compose a children's sermon from Matthew 13:45-46. It was not a lot to go on, but I tried to find a way for the children to engage in a search for a pearl of great value. Since pearls are usually found in oysters, I went to the local grocery store and bought a dozen oysters still in the shell. I rigged them so they were easy to open, and I forced a small pearl into one of the oysters. When the children came to the front of the church for children's time, we opened oysters together, looking for pearls. Finally, we opened one with a pearl, and the children were so excited that our search had been successful; we had found our own pearl of great value. They were not asked to recall feelings of searching and finding from their memories or told about my encounters with searching and finding. The children experienced the thrill of searching and joy of finding, which Jesus emphasized in Luke 15. These feelings can also be evoked by good storytelling and drama; but unlike what happens in storytelling, the children become a physical part of this story, and unlike what happens in drama, the children are themselves rather than the characters they portray.

I recall that particular children's sermon not for the idea I used, but for the feedback I received afterward. A father of two of the children at the children's sermon relayed to me the conversation that occurred on the drive home from the service. He and his wife were discussing the points of the senior minister's sermon when a voice from the backseat vaulted over into the fray. Their daughter recalled her experience with the search and added a new dimension to the family's faith journey. The children's sermon has a much greater value when seen as an integrated part of the entire service rather than when used as a break in the action to address the kids before they can be sent elsewhere.

The ritual dimension of our worship service is our faith community's theology in action. Ritual moves faith from the mind to the body as our ideas about God not only are thought out, but also become reality. A trip to the local science museum finds children running and jumping while learning about science. Discovering gravity and finding out about surface tension are not dull chores, but exciting experiences as the children are encouraged to drop things from various heights and make bubbles of all sizes. The cognitive development abilities of children are considered as this type of science education provides a playground for the senses. Learning about God can be just as exciting and experiential. We must begin to address children on their level instead of keeping them in the pew queue waiting for the time when they, too, can sit back and consume rather than produce worship. Liturgy has become the work of the clergy. Children, however, are not afraid to carry their part of the liturgical load.

Adults often see fastening their seat belts as a chore. My children see it as a game to test who can be buckled up the fastest. Now, it is not a case of whether or not to buckle my seat belt, but of how I can play this safety game with my kids. They have invited and encouraged me to do something that I may have failed to do myself. Children can play the same deconstructionist role for us in worship as they invite all of us into new experiences of God by their playfulness, informality, honesty, and willingness to explore.

When people recall meaningful worship services, they seldom use the language "I heard" or "I saw" the presence of God; rather, the sense of God is felt, experienced. We know God by participating in the text. Looking back to the first Gospel text in Advent, Year B, we ask the question, "How can we make this text accessible to children through their senses?" To find a multisensory experience, it helps to read the text with all the senses in mind. "Senses help us to think and react emotionally."[6] We taste the gospel at Communion, touch the gospel during baptism, and smell the gospel through the burning of incense.

Read Mark 13:24-37 again and make a list of what you sense from the text and what someone who was standing there listening to Jesus might have sensed.

- Sights: Clouds, falling stars, the gates, angels in heaven, Father, Son, Son of Man, darkness, doorkeeper watching for the Master
- Sounds: Cockcrow, keep awake, alarm, a ticking clock
- Tastes: Figs
- Smells: Fig trees, storm, winds
- Touches: Shaking, winds, gathering people, texture of fig leaves
- Feelings: Fear, waiting

25

Since we are forced to begin with a print medium, the Scriptures, sight and hearing are the givens for any sermon or children's sermon. The key is to layer as many senses within the children's sermon as possible, using taste, smell, and touch whenever possible. Even multimedia and virtual reality have not adequately included these senses in ways of which we are capable in the worship setting.

If we retain less than 15 percent of what we hear, oral sermons are like homiletical billboards posted all along the highway, seldom remembered or responded to beyond an immediate reaction. The task in creating a children's sermon is to discover what the children can do to experience the text rather than what they can be told about the text. Word pictures are no longer our primary means of communication.

When asked what they learned in school that day, young children primarily recount what they did, not what they learned. Children are doers! Their perceptions of what they do know are often distorted as one child in my first church recalled, "Mama, I do know my ABC's. It's just that my ABC's are different from your ABC's." Children learn the alphabet song and assume they know the alphabet. My children thought LMNO was a word, not a series of letters. Just because children can tell you they have learned something doesn't mean they can use it or apply it.

The intent of the children's sermon is to get children, as well as adults, thinking in new ways. Give children the text in a way they can understand. Allow them to discover the text and find meaning from the experience itself. Be willing to struggle with the loss of control as you are no longer making a point for the children or making points with the parents, but joining the children on a journey into the text and into faith.

Outline of the Methodology for Experiencing the Gospel

I. Select the Scripture text to be shared with the children.

A. Exegete the text. Decide if the children can connect in some way to the text. Note: not all texts are accessible to children.

B. If at all possible, use the same text to be used with the adults.

II. Identify preparatory postures within the text.

A. Assume at least one of the postures you have identified.

B. Move into the text physically in order to prepare for interaction with the children.

C. Have fun; remember this is a playful posture.

III. Search for sensory stimuli in the text.

A. List the stimuli as found in the five sensory categories:
1. Sight
2. Sound
3. Taste
4. Smell
5. Touch

B. Identify the senses that can be re-created in the worship setting.

C. Identify which of these senses will connect the experiences of children to the text.
1. Observe children in their interactions; listen to their language; taste the current fad food popular with children.
2. Use all of your senses to prepare.

IV. **Bring the text to life with a multisensory experience.**

    A. Attempt to use three or more senses.
    B. Allow the children to participate rather than observe.
    C. Ask open-ended questions to help the children reflect on their experience.

V. **Link the children's sermon to the adult's sermon and the entire worship service.**

    A. Use the same Scripture text (if possible).
    B. Invite the adults into an experience.
    C. Discuss with the entire congregation any questions that emerged from the children's sermon.

FIRST SUNDAY OF ADVENT
LECTIONARY READINGS:
Isaiah 2:1-5
Psalm 122
Romans 13:11-14
Matthew 24: 36-44

TEXT: Matthew 24: 36-44

PREPARATORY POSTURE: Visit a place where people usually wait, such as a hospital emergency room or a bus station. Observe the rituals of waiting. Practice or learn a magic trick.

EXPERIENCE: The intention of this experience is to create an atmosphere of anticipation rather than merely discuss the feelings that arise from waiting. Begin by giving the children clues about what to watch for during the Advent season, including the changes in the sanctuary and the liturgy. Explain that Advent is a time to wait and watch for Jesus. Talk about the ways we wait. Let them complete the phrase, "I can hardly wait until _____." Enlist a budding or self-taught magician from your congregation to perform a magic trick for the children. Be sure that the trick creates a sense of anticipation and requires careful observation and concentration. Letting the children turn the crank of a jack-in-the-box could also be used to create the sensation of the need to be ready.

Note: Magic stores often carry a line of easy-to-learn Christian magic tricks. To order such tricks directly, write: Dock Haley, 1705 Barbara Lane, Connersville, IN 47331

SENSES: *Hearing, sight, and touch*

SECOND SUNDAY OF ADVENT
LECTIONARY READINGS:
Isaiah 11:1-10
Psalm 72:1-7, 18-19
Romans 15:4-13
Matthew 3:1-12

TEXT: Matthew 3:1-12

PREPARATORY POSTURE: Carry an egg around with you each day. Protect it from harm.

EXPERIENCE: Show the children pictures of an apple or another kind of fruit from the moment the blossom first appears to the time the fruit is ready to be picked. Ask the children to identify things that could keep the fruit from ever being eaten. Frost, insects, birds, and disease are the major ones.

Ask the children, "What kinds of things do you think could get in your way of being disciples of Jesus as you grow older?"

Discuss with the children the challenges of peer pressure and the need to "fit in" and how this could get in their way of being disciples of Jesus.

Give each child an unripe piece of fruit to protect for a few days as it ripens. Encourage them to bring their fruit safely back the next week.

Prepare a fruit salad for the children to share after worship. For a quick and easy fruit salad combine apples, pears, and strawberries. You could also sprinkle a little sugar over the fruit or eat it plain and enjoy the fruit's natural sweetness. If possible, have the kids help with preparing the salad.

SENSES: *Hearing, sight, smell, taste, and touch*

THIRD SUNDAY OF ADVENT
LECTIONARY READINGS:
Isaiah 35:1-10
Luke 1:47-55
James 5:7-10
Matthew 11:2-11

TEXT: Isaiah 35:1-10

PREPARATORY POSTURE: Walk up and down the streets or roads of your community and look for those who are fearful in heart and need signs of joy and hope. Identify ways to extend God's Holy Way outside the aisles of your sanctuary.

EXPERIENCE: This Sunday, prepare a joyous Advent parade as you lead the children on a trip along the Holy Way. Designate an aisle or area in the church as the Holy Way. Black paper with dashed yellow lines down the center makes an instant highway that can easily be rolled out and rolled back up. Blindfold some of the travelers. Cover the mouths and ears of others. Make it difficult for some to walk by tying their shoelaces together. Then read the scripture passage from Isaiah as other members of the congregation open the travelers' eyes, ears, and mouths. Untie the shoelace-bound and encourage them to leap in the air. Lead everyone down the Holy Way. When the procession gets to the other end, place stickers or pieces of tape with the word *Joy* written on them on the travelers' heads. Sing songs of joy as they celebrate their return along the Holy Way.

SENSES: *Hearing, sight, and touch*

FOURTH SUNDAY OF ADVENT
LECTIONARY READINGS:
Isaiah 7:10-16

Psalm 80:1-7, 17-19

Romans 1:1-7

Matthew 1:18-25

TEXT: Matthew 1:18-25

PREPARATORY POSTURE: Write down a list of the things you truly want for Christmas. Share your dreams with someone close to you.

EXPERIENCE: Ask each child, "What do you want for Christmas?" Then, using a dry erase board or large sheets of paper, let children make a list of what they think Jesus would want for Christmas. Tell the children that you have read the Bible and know what is on Jesus' list. Show the children Jesus' Christmas list, which contains only one word, *YOU*. Jesus wants us to love God and follow God's rules for our lives, just as Joseph did. God's gift to us is God, Emmanuel, "God with us." To help children remember God's gift to us, prepare a big wrapped box. Ask everyone who wants to be part of Jesus' Christmas gift to step inside the box, or put a gift tag and perhaps a bow on each child who wants to be on Jesus' Christmas list. Let the children fill out the tags—To: Jesus; From: *[Insert Child's Name]*.

Children will enjoy hearing the story of Joseph's dream. Ask the children what they would like to name a child. Tell how Joseph was told Jesus' name in a dream. Be prepared to define terms such as *conceived* and *virgin* if you use them in your story. Explain how you got your name. Encourage the children to go home and ask their parents about their names.

SENSES: *Hearing, sight, and touch*

32

FIRST SUNDAY AFTER CHRISTMAS DAY
LECTIONARY READINGS:
Isaiah 63:7-9
Psalm 148
Hebrews 2:10-18
Matthew 2:13-23

TEXT: Matthew 2:13-23

PREPARATORY POSTURE: Visit the local library or search the Internet for articles on the major events of the past year. Review significant events in your life and the world over the past twelve months.

EXPERIENCE: Help the children think back through things that have happened in the past year to them, to their families, to the church, and to the world. Include pictures of major world events and activities around the church for them to identify. Make a list of things that were helpful and things that were hurtful. Be open to the possibilities for pastoral care in this exercise.

Create a litany with a simple response so the children can recall both the good and the bad of the past year. Discuss their hopes and fears for the coming year.

Ask the children to play the parts of Joseph, Mary, the angel, and Jesus as we find the angel coming to Joseph in a dream again. Getting away safely was a good thing, but a bad thing followed. Children who have seen such scenes as the Oklahoma bombing can cope with the retelling of Herod's killing in and around Bethlehem. Explain what happened while Joseph, Mary, and Jesus were in Egypt; and continue the role play as Joseph is again told in a dream to leave Egypt, to come back to Israel, and to settle in Nazareth.

SENSES: *Hearing and sight*

33

EPIPHANY OF THE LORD

LECTIONARY READINGS:

Isaiah 60:1-6

Psalm 72:1-7, 10-14

Ephesians 3:1-12

Matthew 2:1-12

TEXT: Matthew 2:1-12

PREPARATORY POSTURE: Go outside at night and lie down on a blanket to look up at the stars. Identify the brightest stars and any planets and constellations you recognize. If you live in a city where it is difficult to see the stars, visit your local planetarium.

EXPERIENCE: Read the Gospel passage from Matthew. Answer any questions the children might have about the story. Hold up a star and ask the children to follow the star all around the sanctuary until they get to the place where Jesus is. This could be the manger scene, the cross, the baptismal font, or any number of places. Use more than one example of where Jesus is present today.

For small churches: Invite the children to join you under a blanket or another tentlike structure to look at the stars. Use the glow-in-the-dark stars that are designed for ceilings to create the effect of a starscape in the dark created by the blanket.

For large churches: Give away glow-in-the-dark stars for the children to take home and place on their bedroom ceilings to remind them of the wise men's search for the baby Jesus.

SENSES: *Hearing, sight, and touch*

BAPTISM OF THE LORD (First Sunday After the Epiphany)
LECTIONARY READINGS:
Isaiah 42:1-9
Psalm 29
Acts 10:34-43
Matthew 3:13-17

TEXT: Mark 1:4-11

PREPARATORY POSTURE: Write a letter to the person who baptized you, updating what has transpired since that time. If the person is still living, send it to him or her. If not, discuss it with someone who has not been baptized.

EXPERIENCE: Baptism of the Lord Sunday provides an opportunity to teach children about baptism. Walk the children through a baptismal ceremony without actually using water. Pretend to let the water fall through your fingers, and answer any questions the children have about your church tradition. Then ask if any of the children would like to baptize you. Some will be more than willing, but the ones who are hesitant can be compared to John the Baptist, who must have shaken his head in disbelief at Jesus' request to be baptized. Allow the children to pretend to baptize you. Ask the children if they know who baptized them. If they do not know or have not been baptized, suggest that they discuss baptism with their families. Be sure to emphasize that John baptized Jesus. Give older children an envelope and a piece of paper to write a note to the person who baptized them. The letter should give the baptizer an update on their Christian life. Conclude worship with a service of baptismal remembrance.

SENSES: *Hearing, sight, and touch*

SECOND SUNDAY AFTER THE EPIPHANY
LECTIONARY READINGS:
Isaiah 49:1-7

Psalm 40:1-11

1 Corinthians 1:1-9

John 1:29-42

TEXT: John 1:29-42

PREPARATORY POSTURE: Go on a scavenger hunt or prepare a scavenger hunt for several children. Help them find all the items on their lists.

EXPERIENCE: Invite the children to go on a scavenger hunt. Give them one item to look for: "God." Send them out into the sanctuary to find something that reminds them of God/Jesus/the Holy Spirit. Encourage the children to explain their selections to the congregation. Invite the entire congregation to return next week with reminders of God that they find and to share these with their fellow worshipers so that all might say, "We have found the Messiah."

For the risk taker: Send the children out at the beginning of the service with instructions to return by the end of the service with as many reminders of God as they can find. Allow them to go outside and all around the church to find things that remind them of God.

SENSES: *Hearing, sight, and touch*

THIRD SUNDAY AFTER THE EPIPHANY
LECTIONARY READINGS:
Isaiah 9:1-4

Psalm 27:1, 4-9

1 Corinthians 1:10-18
Matthew 4:12-23

TEXT: 1 Corinthians 1:10-18

PREPARATORY POSTURE: Put together a jigsaw puzzle.

EXPERIENCE: Select a jigsaw puzzle with a few more pieces than you will have children participating in the children's sermon. Give each child a puzzle piece while purposely holding back a few key pieces. Help the children put the puzzle together. Discuss the difficulty of not having all the pieces and the importance of each individual piece. Give the children the rest of the pieces and complete the puzzle. God wants to use all the pieces, all of God's people, to make complete pictures.

Games without all the pieces can also be a useful image for children.

To examine the competing factions that Paul is addressing, children might be asked about their favorite football teams as the Super Bowl approaches. Kids can be divided by teams they root for, but that should not keep them apart. As Christians, we are united by the cross. Use a cross like a magnet to draw everyone back together. In some larger churches, local rivalries between schools can also be used.

SENSES: *Hearing, sight, and touch*

FOURTH SUNDAY AFTER THE EPIPHANY
LECTIONARY READINGS:
Micah 6:1-8
Psalm 15
1 Corinthians 1:18-31
Matthew 5:1-12

TEXT: 1 Corinthians 1:18-31

PREPARATORY POSTURE: Recall a cheer from your school days. Yell it out as a cheer. Watch or attend a football or basketball game and take part in the cheering.

EXPERIENCE: A friend once said that there is too much booing in our churches and not enough cheering. Help your church develop some new cheers with the help of the children. They will be familiar with spelling cheers: Gimme a C. C! Gimme an H. H! Let the children lead the liturgical wave as it flows back and forth across the congregation. Cheer the Beatitudes with the children by letting them yell or say, "Blessed are . . .," and having others from the congregation complete the phrases from their Bibles. Try, "Three cheers for the poor in spirit." "Blessed, Blessed, Blessed!" These are strange-sounding cheers, so discuss some examples of when Christians should cheer.

SENSES: *Hearing, sight, and touch*

FIFTH SUNDAY AFTER THE EPIPHANY
LECTIONARY READINGS:
Isaiah 58:1-9*a* (9*b*-12)
Psalm 112:1-9 (10)
1 Corinthians 2:1-12 (13-16)
Matthew 5:13-20

TEXT: Matthew 5:13-20

PREPARATORY POSTURE: By letter, phone, or in person, thank someone who has guided you spiritually.

EXPERIENCE: We all have people to whom we look for

guidance. Children can identify those persons by answering, "If you were going out to look for God, who would you want to take with you?" Close the service or the children's time by inviting the children to bring their guides/fellow travelers with them to the front of the church. Many of those who see themselves as "hiding their lights under a bushel" will be considered to be "lamps" by the children. Commission these teams to search for God together.

SENSES: *Hearing, sight, and touch*

SIXTH SUNDAY AFTER THE EPIPHANY
LECTIONARY READINGS:
Deuteronomy 30:15-20
Psalm 119:1-8
1 Corinthians 3:1-9
Matthew 5:21-37

TEXT: Deuteronomy 30:15-20

PREPARATORY POSTURE: Make a valentine for someone. Use the images of the cross and a heart to show both God's love and your love for that person.

EXPERIENCE: Ask the children to bring someone they love with them to the children's sermon. (The hope is that these will be adults who can help with this activity.) Prepare folded pieces of paper with the outline of half a heart on one side. Inside the heart, draw the outline of half a cross. With the help of other adults, cut out hearts for each of the children; then from the hearts, cut out the crosses. Let the children place their hearts on the altar and hold fast to their crosses. God shows God's love for us not by a heart-shaped valentine, but by the cross.

SENSES: *Hearing, sight, and touch*

LAST SUNDAY AFTER THE EPIPHANY
(Transfiguration Sunday)
LECTIONARY READINGS:
Exodus 24:12-18
Psalm 99
2 Peter 1:16-21
Matthew 17:1-9

TEXTS: Exodus 24:12-18; 17:9-12

PREPARATORY POSTURE: Extend your arms and hold them in the air for as long as you can.

EXPERIENCE: One of the best examples of teamwork in the Bible comes from Exodus 17:9-12. In this story, we are shown how the team is an integral part of Moses' and Joshua's success. Aaron and Hur were an early tag team who helped Moses keep his hands in the air even when he had grown tired.

Ask a member of the congregation to play Moses, and allow the children to be Aaron and Hur for the rest of the service. Let the children alternate as they are charged with the responsibility of keeping Moses' hands raised until the benediction.

SENSES: *Hearing, sight, and touch*

FIRST SUNDAY IN LENT
LECTIONARY READINGS:
Genesis 2:15-17; 3:1-7

40

Psalm 32
Romans 5:12-19
Matthew 4:1-11

TEXT: Matthew 4:1-11

PREPARATORY POSTURE: Fast for forty hours.

EXPERIENCE: Ask the children if they are hungry or thirsty. Tell them that today is the beginning of Lent when we spend forty days getting ready for Easter. Explain that Lent lasts forty days because Jesus was led by the Spirit into the wilderness where he fasted for forty days and forty nights. Ask the children if they know what it means to fast. Explain fasting and inquire how long it has been since they have eaten. Could they wait forty days? Suggest they wait forty minutes to eat lunch after church and use that time to think or talk about Jesus and Lent with their families.

While Jesus was fasting, the devil came to him and asked him to turn stones into bread. Point to a pile of stones you have gathered. Display cue cards to help the children respond in the way Jesus did. Then ask the children to close their eyes and imagine being on top of the church building. Tell them to open their eyes for the second response. Finally, encourage them to imagine sitting on the highest mountain in the world and let them use the third response. Give them cards with these verses on them to study during Lent. Explain that the devil left Jesus because Jesus could not be tempted to follow him.

SENSES: *Touch, hearing, and sight*

SECOND SUNDAY IN LENT
LECTIONARY READINGS:
Genesis 12:1-4*a*
Psalm 121
Romans 4:1-5, 13-17
John 3:1-17

TEXT: Genesis 12:1-4*a*

PREPARATORY POSTURE: Visit one of your former homes or look through pictures of places you have lived. Recall the difficulties of moving.

EXPERIENCE: Begin by singing and moving with the song "Father Abraham/Mother Sarah."

> Father Abraham had many children,
>   many children had Father Abraham.
> I am one of them and so are you,
> So let's just praise the Lord!

> Right arm. (Everyone starts to swing the right arm, and the song continues.)

Alternate "Mother Sarah" with "Father Abraham," as Royeece Stowe of Covington, Georgia, always reminds us to do.

Movements are added with each verse and include "left arm ... right foot ... left foot ... chin up ... chin down ... turn around ... sit down."

Get everyone moving!

Abraham was forced to get moving to be about God's business, and God was with Abraham and Sarah when they were moving. Talk with the children about times when they have moved. Be prepared to deal with the pain associated with divorce as children may have moved without one of their parents. Other children have experienced the joy and sorrow of older siblings leaving home. For children who

42

have never moved, ask them how they would feel if God told them to move away as God told Abraham and Sarah to do.

SENSES: *Hearing, sight, and touch*

THIRD SUNDAY IN LENT
LECTIONARY READINGS:
Exodus 17:1-7
Psalm 95
Romans 5:1-11
John 4:5-42

TEXT: Exodus 17:1-7

PREPARATORY POSTURE: Drink eight glasses of water every day this week. Use a different glass each day.

EXPERIENCE: Find several clean containers that would appear to be unappetizing from which to drink. Be sure these containers are not clear. Fill the containers with water, and invite the children to drink from them. You might have a few brave kids, but most will shake their heads, "No!" Turn away from the children and pour the water into more appealing containers that are also not clear. Invite them to drink again. Finally, pour the water into transparent glasses with the water clearly displayed. Make sure that you have enough water and containers so that everyone can have a drink. Discuss why the presentation is so important when inviting people to try new things. The Israelites had followed Moses out into the wilderness and had to be shown that the water really was there and that God was faithful even when the people fought among themselves and tested God.

SENSES: *Hearing, sight, smell, taste, and touch*

FOURTH SUNDAY IN LENT
LECTIONARY READINGS:
1 Samuel 16:1-13
Psalm 23
Ephesians 5:8-14
John 9:1-41

TEXT: John 9:1-41

PREPARATORY POSTURE: Gather several children and make mud pies together.

EXPERIENCE: The shortest verse in the Bible could have been "Jesus spit." Kids will love to find out that even Jesus spit. Ask the children if it is okay to spit in church. They will tell you it is not permitted, but you can assure them that Jesus spit—although that doesn't mean you want them to spit in church! Tell the story of the man born without sight whom Jesus heals. Spit into a bowl of dirt and make some mud between your fingers. Then ask for volunteers to have mud on their eyes. Discourage any volunteers. You may want to use a mannequin head to actually put mud on the eyes. Use another bowl of water labeled Siloam to wash the mud from the eyes (and your hands). Discuss what kind of trust it must have taken for the man to allow mud made from spit to be put on his eyes. Ask, "Why didn't people believe that the man had been healed?"

SENSES: *Hearing, sight, taste, and touch*

FIFTH SUNDAY IN LENT
LECTIONARY READINGS:
Ezekiel 37:1-14
Psalm 130

Romans 8:6-11
John 11:1-45

TEXT: John 11:1-45

PREPARATORY POSTURE: Let someone wrap you in clear plastic wrap and then unbind you.

EXPERIENCE: This story begs to be acted out by the children. Cast this miniplay using all the children. Use other members of the congregation if necessary.

Cast:
Lazarus
Messenger who takes Martha's message to Jesus
Mary
Martha
Jesus
The disciples
Thomas

Start with Lazarus and send him off to be bound up while the rest of the story transpires. (A clear plastic packing wrap that sticks only to itself works perfectly for this. Keep the wrap away from the child's face and have adults do the binding.) Give the disciples and the rest of the congregation specific actions to perform such as holding their noses whenever Lazarus is mentioned. Read through the text from beginning to end with the finale being Lazarus' unbinding.

Discuss with the children their reactions to the story, especially Jesus' crying. Ask, "Do you believe Jesus cried?" Talk with Mary and Martha about their reactions. Ask Lazarus how it felt to be unbound.

SENSES: *Hearing, sight, smell, and touch*

PASSION/PALM SUNDAY
LECTIONARY READINGS:
Isaiah 50:4-9*a*
Psalm 31:9-16 or Psalm 118:1-2, 19-29
Philippians 2:5-11
Matthew 26:14–27:66, Matthew 27:11-54, or Matthew 21:1-11

TEXT: Matthew 21:1-11

PREPARATORY POSTURE: Ride a donkey or a horse. Experiment with ways of riding on two animals at once with the youth that are suggested for the following experience.

EXPERIENCE: Matthew's attempt to fulfill the Old Testament prophecies finds us with two animals in chapter 21. The disciples are instructed to go into town and find a donkey and a colt. Send two children out to find the donkey and the colt, which can be played by two volunteers from the senior high youth who have been forewarned of their roles. Ask another youth to act as the guard for these steeds. When the children try to untie them, let the guard ask them what they are doing. All the children can respond, "The Lord needs them." The guard can then send the donkey and the colt to Jesus and the other disciples.

The difficulty will come when the children lay a cloak across the backs of the animals and the child playing the role of Jesus attempts to sit on them. How can you ride two animals? Try the different variations that the kids suggest. Perhaps Jesus stood with one foot on each animal, and it created a parade atmosphere. Provide cloaks and palm branches for the road, and let the two animals and the child playing Jesus travel across them while the rest of the children shout, "Hosanna to the Son of David! Blessed is the one who comes in the name of the Lord! Hosanna in the highest heaven!"

SENSES: *Hearing, sight, and touch*

EASTER DAY
LECTIONARY READINGS:
Acts 10:34-43
Psalm 118:1-2, 14-24
Colossians 3:1-4
Matthew 28:1-10 or John 20:1-18

TEXT: John 20:1-18

PREPARATORY POSTURE: Wake up while it is still dark outside. Run to a nearby cemetery. Watch the sun rise.

EXPERIENCE: The excitement and apprehension of the disciples on Easter Day can be re-created among the children. One of the cardinal rules of most sanctuaries and churches is *no running.* Imagine people running up the aisle to join the church or running to the altar to take Communion! A pastor in Pine Mountain, Georgia, took the risk of giving children permission to run in church on this special day because the joy of the Resurrection calls for a full gallop, not a trot. The story begins with Mary's running to tell Simon Peter and the other disciple that the stone had been removed. Then Peter and another disciple were running to the tomb, but the other disciple outran Peter.

Divide the children into pairs and let them run a race from the back of the sanctuary to the front. Take all the children who lost their heats and identify them with Peter. While reminding them of the empty tomb, allow them to go to a special place in the sanctuary, such as the altar, where they can examine linen wrapping that has been rolled up. Then invite the winners to join you as you continue the discussion of the empty tomb. Depending upon the size of the group and the abundance of Easter dresses, you may want to use several of the girls to play the part of Mary Magdalene. Her role is to act as a starting gun by running to tell others the news and by providing the subsequent weeping.

SENSES: *Hearing, sight, and touch*

SECOND SUNDAY OF EASTER
LECTIONARY READINGS:
Acts 2:14*a*, 22-32
Psalm 16
1 Peter 1:3-9
John 20:19-31

TEXT: John 20:19-31

PREPARATORY POSTURE: Take a deep breath. Hold it as long as you can.

EXPERIENCE: Jesus appears among the disciples and says, "Peace be with you." Then he does something many children and most adults will find almost repulsive. He breathes on them. He breathes on them, and they receive the Holy Spirit. Ask the children if they would want to have someone breathe on them. (The strongest breath would certainly be a weakness at this point!) Ask if they would want Jesus to breathe on them. Pass out breath mints to remind all the children that Jesus breathed on the disciples and they received something wonderful from that action, the Holy Spirit.

A dummy that is used to teach mouth-to-mouth resuscitation might also be an effective way to show the power of breath in giving life. CPR instructors will relish the opportunity to get children interested in the lifesaving method. Use this as a springboard to begin a CPR training class.

SENSES: *Hearing, sight, smell, taste, and touch*

THIRD SUNDAY OF EASTER
LECTIONARY READINGS:
Acts 2:14*a*, 36-41
Psalm 116:1-4, 12-19
1 Peter 1:17-23
Luke 24:13-35

TEXT: Luke 24:13-35

PREPARATORY POSTURE: Share a meal with someone you have not seen for a while. Be sure to share a fresh loaf of bread.

EXPERIENCE: Take the children through a pantomime of all the ways people around the world get to church. Ask for their suggestions; use everything from cars and feet to boats, airplanes, and dog sleds. Sing the song "Give Me Oil in My Lamp." Include all the transportation verses.

> Give me:
> Gas for my Ford, keep me trucking for the Lord.
> Wax for my board, keep me surfing for the Lord.
> Hay for my mule, let me get to Sunday school.
> Jesus in my life, keep me free from sin and strife.

Give all the kids tickets to ride with Jesus who didn't have a one-way ticket to death, but had a round-trip ticket to life. Jesus walked the road to Emmaus and continues to travel with us. Break bread with the children and recall the words of Jesus so they, too, might begin recognizing Jesus in the breaking of the bread.

SENSES: *Hearing, sight, touch, smell, and taste*

FOURTH SUNDAY OF EASTER
LECTIONARY READINGS:
Acts 2:42-47
Psalm 23
1 Peter 2:19-25
John 10:1-10

TEXT: 1 Peter 2:19-25

PREPARATORY POSTURE: Go dancing. Learn a new dance step.

EXPERIENCE: Some children will be familiar with footprints that are used to teach dance steps. Place some footprints on the floor in a common dance pattern and see if the children can follow the steps. An easy dance step to teach without footprints would be the bunny hop to the tune of "Lord of the Dance." A couple of verses bear repeating in the Easter season:

> They buried my body and they thought I'd gone,
> but I am the dance and I still go on.

Prepare another set of footsteps leading to the sanctuary cross, and ask the children to follow them. Arrange the footsteps so that they go all the way up the side of the wall to the cross. We are called to follow in Jesus' steps, but we cannot always follow the exact same way to the cross.

SENSES: *Hearing, sight, and touch*

FIFTH SUNDAY OF EASTER
LECTIONARY READINGS:
Acts 7:55-60
Psalm 31:1-5, 15-16
1 Peter 2:2-10
John 14:1-14

TEXT: John 15:1-8

PREPARATORY POSTURE: Make a rubbing of a corner-stone in your community. An unwrapped crayon works well.

EXPERIENCE: A cornerstone often encloses a time capsule meant to be opened by future generations. Either let the children help you decide what should be included in a time capsule to be opened in the future or share with them a time capsule you have "discovered" that was left for them by an earlier generation of the church. This could date back as far as the disciples or back to the founding of your congregation. Use old pictures to show children about the way things were. Many churches celebrate Homecoming on the first Sunday in May, and this would be a perfect way to involve children in the reminiscing. If you choose to make a time capsule with the children, give them the opportunity to bring items to place in the box. Take instant photographs of the children and include them. Be sure to place the date on the box when it will be opened.

SENSES: *Hearing, sight, and touch*

SIXTH SUNDAY OF EASTER
LECTIONARY READINGS:
Acts 17:22-31
Psalm 66:8-20

1 Peter 3:13-22
John 14:15-21

TEXT: Acts 17:22-31

PREPARATORY POSTURE: Write a note to your mother.

EXPERIENCE: Tell the children there is a special gift for each of their mothers somewhere in the sanctuary. Invite them to search for the special gifts. Give them clues, such as, "The gifts are easily visible," or "The gifts shouldn't be hard for you to find." Send them out to search. You could also use the "you're getting warmer" technique with a small group. The gifts for the mothers are the children themselves. The children will look elsewhere when the most special gifts were right under their noses. Just as we are thankful to be God's offspring, we are thankful to be the offspring of our parents.

SENSES: *Hearing, sight, and touch*

ASCENSION OF THE LORD/SEVENTH SUNDAY OF EASTER
LECTIONARY READINGS:
Acts 1:1-11/Acts 1:6-14
Psalm 47/Psalm 68:1-10, 32-35
Ephesians 1:15-23/1 Peter 4:12-14; 5:6-11
Luke 24:44-53/John 17:1-11

TEXT: 1 Peter 4:12-14; 5:6-11

PREPARATORY POSTURE: Look up in the sky. Examine the clouds. Imagine Jesus being lifted up and one of those clouds taking him from your sight.

EXPERIENCE: Ask the children to stay alert and be ready for anything. Arrange ahead of time for someone to dress in a lion costume and pounce onto the scene. Or use a lion's roar through the PA system to gather all the children behind you. Play the role of the lion tamer, holding up a wooden chair to protect the children as the lion prowls around. Talk about their fears and reassure them that God will protect them. God will stand between them and any challenges because "God cares for you."

The roaring lion from verse 8 sounds like Scar from the Walt Disney movie, *The Lion King*. Contrast the instructions in 1 Peter to the instructions given to the hyenas by Scar. Play the song "Be Prepared," sung by Scar (Jeremy Irons) in *The Lion King*, and then talk about what the words mean. A word of caution. This is copyrighted material and you will need permission if you plan to reprint it.

SENSES: *Hearing, sight, and touch*

DAY OF PENTECOST
LECTIONARY READINGS:
Acts 2:1-21
Psalm 104:24-34, 35*b*
1 Corinthians 12:3*b*-13
John 7:37-39

TEXT: Acts 2:1-21

PREPARATORY POSTURE: Fly a kite! Let the wind take the kite as high as it can.

EXPERIENCE: Spirit banners often make appearances at high school football games. A huge piece of paper is tied between two poles and painted with team colors and hopes of victory. The cheerleaders hold the banner in the air between them and run down the field to the spot where it is set up for the football players to burst through. One of the keys to making a good spirit banner is cutting holes in strategic places so that the act of running down the field is even possible. Holes allow the wind to blow through the banner as the messengers run with it. Cheerleaders sometimes learn the necessity of holes the hard way as they try to run with their banner unfurled only to have the banner rip or slow their run to a walk. Make spirit banners with or for the children to celebrate Pentecost. Allow them to run up and down the aisles of the church with the spirit banners unfurled, have a pep rally during Sunday school, or clear the parking lot for a victory run right after worship. Let the children burst through the banner, and remind them of the way the Holy Spirit burst into the room on the day of Pentecost.

SENSES: *Hearing, sight, and touch*

TRINITY SUNDAY
LECTIONARY READINGS:
Genesis 1:1–2:4*a*
Psalm 8
2 Corinthians 13:11-13
Matthew 28:16-20

TEXTS: Genesis 1:1–2:4*a*; 2 Corinthians 13:11-13

PREPARATORY POSTURE: Sleep in a sleeping bag.

EXPERIENCE: Why is it that no child ever stays tucked in? Our children want to be tucked in two and three times some evenings. Encourage all the children to pretend to be asleep. Zip one child tightly in a sleeping bag from which she or he will need help to escape. Tuck in another child using a simple cover and perhaps a holy kiss good night. As the children "sleep," share with them messages of God's love and peace. When we know God's love for us, we want to be able to get up and share that with others. Leonard Sweet in the preaching resources, *Homiletics Preaching Resource*, tells of a mother who tells her daughters to "sleep loose" instead of sleep tight. She encourages them to trust God's love for them even as they sleep. If we try to protect ourselves too much, like what happens when we use a sleeping bag, we can't get out to share the good news with others.

Tell the children about Paul's letter to the Corinthians and how he is telling them good-bye. How do they say good-bye? Why are good-byes important?

You might want to share the Genesis text with the children, putting them to bed each night and waking them up with each new day. The frustration of trying to get out of the sleeping bag is increased if all seven days are used.

SENSES: *Hearing, sight, and touch*

SUNDAY BETWEEN MAY 29 AND JUNE 4 INCLUSIVE
LECTIONARY READINGS:
(If After Trinity Sunday)
Genesis 6:9-22; 7:24; 8:14-19
Psalm 46
Romans 1:16-17; 3:22*b*-28, (29-31)
Matthew 7:21-29

TEXT: Genesis 6:9-22; 7:24; 8:14-19

PREPARATORY POSTURE: Visit a factory that makes boats or go to a marina. Look at all the different types of boats. Find out how boats are made today. Watch the weather channel.

EXPERIENCE: Help the children imagine what it was like for Noah to build the ark. Write out God's instructions to Noah on a large piece of paper or on a chalkboard for the children to see.

1. Make an ark of gopher wood.
2. Make rooms.
3. Cover it inside and out with pitch. (Explain what pitch is or show them some.)
4. Make the ark:
   300 cubits long, approximately 450 feet
    50 cubits wide, approximately 75 feet
    30 cubits high, approximately 45 feet

   (Explain that a cubit is the length of a forearm from the elbow to the tip of the middle finger. See how many cubits the children have among them.)

5. Make a roof and finish it.
6. Set a door in the side of the ark.
7. Make three decks.
8. Take your family with you (eight passengers).
9. Take two of every living thing (for example, birds, animals, and creeping things). Allow the children to name some animals they would take.
10. Take with you every sort of food that is eaten. Allow the children to name the foods they would take.

Help the children imagine the Flood, which lasted 150 days. If time permits, take them through a typical day on the ark, sleeping, rising, eating some 150 times. Finally, the earth is dry, and the children leave the boat and go back to their seats.

SENSES: *Hearing, sight, smell, and touch*

PROPER 5

LECTIONARY READINGS:
(If After Trinity Sunday)
Genesis 12:1-9
Psalm 33:1-12
Romans 4:13-25
Matthew 9:9-13, 18-26

TEXT: Matthew 9:9-13, 18-26

PREPARATORY POSTURE: Take your temperature.

EXPERIENCE: Begin by walking through the church, inviting the children to follow you. As they follow you, bring them to the place of the children's sermon. Ask them, "How are you feeling today? Is anyone feeling sick?" Take time to deal with any ailments they might share. Prepare numerous ways to treat them as if they were sick: nurses ready to take their temperatures, doctors for their blood pressure, ice packs for their heads, tongue depressors for "ahs," and anything else that a doctor might do for them when they are sick. Have a doctor there to write prescriptions for each child with notes such as "Read your Bible twice a day,"and so on. Be sure to tell them that God is in the healing business and works with doctors, nurses, and other health care providers to make us well. We are part of a great PPO—Preferred Provider Organization. Let actual doctors and nurses share the ways in which they are called to a ministry of healing.

SENSES: *Hearing, touch, and sight*

PROPER 6

SUNDAY BETWEEN JUNE 12 AND JUNE 18 INCLUSIVE

LECTIONARY READINGS:
(If After Trinity Sunday)
Genesis 18:1-15 (21:1-7)
Psalm 116:1-2, 12-19
Romans 5:1-8
Matthew 9:35–10:8 (9-23)

TEXT: Matthew 9:35–10:8 (9-23)

PREPARATORY POSTURE: Search for a box for a large refrigerator. Try to name the twelve disciples from memory.

EXPERIENCE: Find a large refrigerator box and use it to construct a Disciple-Making Machine. Put a crank that turns on the front and a door on each side. Be sure the doors open away from the congregation. Before the service starts, hide one of the parents (a dad if this happens to be Father's Day) in the box. Feature the children's sermon early in the service! When the children come forward, ask one of the hidden parent's children to get into the box. Turn the crank and open the other door and have the parent walk out to the amazement of the gathered children while the child remains in the box. Making disciples is not this easy, and getting bigger or growing older doesn't make one a disciple. Invite all the parents (or dads) in the church to join the children at the front. Invite them to share what it means to them to be a disciple. Send all the children and the parents out to be disciples. How can your church become a Disciple-Making Machine?

SENSES: *Hearing, touch, and sight*

PROPER 7

SUNDAY BETWEEN JUNE 19 AND JUNE 25 INCLUSIVE

LECTIONARY READINGS:

(If After Trinity Sunday)

Genesis 21:8-21

Psalm 86:1-10, 16-17 or Psalm 69:7-10 (11-15), 16-18

Romans 6:1*b*-11

Matthew 10:24-39

TEXT: Matthew 10:24-39

PREPARATORY POSTURE: Attempt to count the hairs on your head. Get a haircut. Make a list of your favorite things!

EXPERIENCE: On the previous Sunday, ask each child to bring one favorite thing to church. Discuss why they brought each item. Are these things really their favorite things? Did anyone bring a person? What is the meaning of the statement, "The best things in the world are not things"? Ask them, "What are your favorite things about being a Christian?"—a question that might pave the road for the adults to more freely respond to the sermon.

Attempt to count the hairs on one child's head. Use a red-head if possible—they have fewer total follicles. When the children begin to comprehend the immensity of the task, share with them that God loves each of us enough to go to the trouble of counting all the hairs on our heads. (God must certainly be busy during haircuts!) Children are some of God's favorite things! Maybe even God's "most favorite" thing!

SENSES: *Hearing, sight, and touch*

PROPER 8

SUNDAY BETWEEN JUNE 26 AND JULY 2 INCLUSIVE

LECTIONARY READINGS:

Genesis 22:1-14

Psalm 13

Romans 6:12-23

Matthew 10:40-42

TEXT: Matthew 10:40-42

PREPARATORY POSTURE: Share a cup of cold water with someone who looks thirsty.

EXPERIENCE: Sometimes the obvious approach is best. Giving a cup of cold water to the little ones who gather for the children's sermon will be welcomed on a warm summer Sunday. Ask some adults to dress as the disciples and wear name tags of the Twelve. Give each child a cup of ice water, mentioning the name of a disciple. You might use this to start a Cup of Cold Water ministry offered by the church's children, which would offer cold drinks (for example, water, iced tea, lemonade) after church every Sunday for the rest of the summer.

SENSES: *Hearing, sight, taste, and touch*

PROPER 9

SUNDAY BETWEEN JULY 3 AND JULY 9 INCLUSIVE

LECTIONARY READINGS:

Genesis 24:34-38, 42-49, 58-67

Psalm 45:10-17 or Psalm 145:8-14

Romans 7:15-25*a*
Matthew 11:16-19, 25-30

TEXTS: Matthew 11:16-19, 25-30; Genesis 24:34-38, 42-
    49, 58-67

PREPARATORY POSTURE: Visit a spring. Carry some
water home to use this week.

EXPERIENCE: When you say "yoke," children will think you
are speaking of an egg yolk. Show the children what a yoke
actually is and how it was used to distribute a burden between
animals. Then move the discussion to the yoke of obedience,
the pastor's stole. Explain how the pastor is yoked to serve
God, then "yoke" the children by placing brightly colored rib-
bons around their shoulders. Yoke each one with the words,
"Jesus said, . . . 'For my yoke is easy, and my burden is light.' "
    A lesson I learned in childhood was that when my arms
were too tired to carry a heavy object, I could rest it on my
shoulder, distribute the weight between my shoulder and
my hand, and carry the burden for long distances. The
water jug that Rebekah carries on her shoulder could be
used to teach this practical lesson for carrying trays, boxes,
and other heavy items. Children will enjoy the chance to
try carrying things they thought were too heavy.

SENSES: *Hearing, sight, and touch*

PROPER 10

SUNDAY BETWEEN JULY 10 AND JULY 16
INCLUSIVE
LECTIONARY READINGS:
Genesis 25:19-34

Psalm 119:105-12 or Psalm 65:(1-8) 9-13
Romans 8:1-11
Matthew 13:1-9, 18-23

TEXT: Matthew 13:1-9, 18-23

PREPARATORY POSTURE: Plant a flower.

EXPERIENCE: **For large churches:** Provide enough seeds for each child to sow one or two seeds into several large pots containing various types of soil. Tell the parable of the sower and let them predict what will happen in each pot. Tend the seeds during the weeks to come and see what transpires.

For small churches: Provide each child with a clay or plastic pot and several seeds. Encourage them to go home and plant the seeds in any type of soil. Ask the children to care for their plants until school starts. Bring the plants back on a designated Sunday to see what the sowing produced.

Flowers, such as hydrangeas, that react to the acidity of the soil would be great. Be sure to use flowers that will bud in the allotted time period.

SENSES: *Hearing, sight, and touch*

PROPER 11

SUNDAY BETWEEN JULY 17 AND JULY 23 INCLUSIVE
LECTIONARY READINGS:
Genesis 28:10-19*a*
Psalm 139:1-12, 23-24
Romans 8:12-25
Matthew 13:24-30, 36-43

TEXT: Matthew 13:24-30, 36-43

PREPARATORY POSTURE: Pull some weeds.

EXPERIENCE: Instead of handing out business cards, Jim Thomas of Stark, Georgia hands out laminated passes entitling the bearer to free admission to any events going on at his church. Of course, all the events are free, but this church has taken an inviting posture. Supply each child with a stack of invitations to church or to a special event such as vacation Bible school. Ask them who they would like to invite, and help them to expand their lists to people they had not considered. Give them the job of inviting others to participate. We are called to invite others to join in, not to decide who is to be included and excluded.

This would also be a good time to introduce and honor the ushers or greeters who are not guarding the doors to keep certain people out as they would at a sporting event, but who are welcoming everyone into the church.

SENSES: *Hearing, touch, and sight*

SUNDAY BETWEEN JULY 24 AND JULY 30 INCLUSIVE
LECTIONARY READINGS:
Genesis 29:15-28
Psalm 105:1-11, 45*b*
Romans 8:26-39
Matthew 13:31-33, 44-52

TEXT: Romans 8:26-39

PREPARATORY POSTURE: Bake a cake. Mix some epoxy glue.

EXPERIENCE: Help the children to understand that nothing can separate us from the love of God. On one level, nothing can get between God and us because God is everywhere, but on another level, once we get mixed up with God, nothing will break us apart. Put together a mixture that cannot be separated, such as a cake mix. Let the children help mix the cake.

Arrange for someone to bake the cake in a heart-shaped pan during your well-timed sermon. Or you could follow the lead of television cooking shows and have a cake already baked, iced, and decorated rather than bake it during the service. Invite the children to share in this expression of God's great love for them after worship.

Epoxy mixed from two tubes and used to bind something together might also be used as an example.

SENSES: *Hearing, touch, taste, smell, and sight*

PROPER 13

SUNDAY BETWEEN JULY 31 AND AUGUST 6 INCLUSIVE

LECTIONARY READINGS:
Genesis 32:22-31
Psalm 17:1-7, 15
Romans 9:1-5
Matthew 14:13-21

TEXTS: Genesis 32:22-31; Matthew 14:13-21

PREPARATORY POSTURE: Eat a meal of bread and fish.

Pack a lunch this week.

EXPERIENCE: Act out the story of Jacob. You could start with getting up in the middle of the night and packing everything, but be ready to answer questions about his two wives and his two maids. Prepare two children to play the role of Jacob and the angel so that the wrestling does not get out of hand. Help them with the dialogue as you narrate the story. What would the children do if they were given a new name? Why did Jacob/Israel think he was wrestling with God?

This would also be a good Sunday to ask the children what they think about Communion and answer their questions about the body and the blood of Christ. If your tradition allows, serve the children first. Then, trusting God, allow the children to serve the adults. A less risky option is to have each child bring someone he or she trusts to the table with him or her to share in the Eucharist as served by the appropriate person(s).

If Communion is not being shared this Sunday, prepare a basket with five loaves and two fish, and give the children a taste of both.

SENSES: *Hearing, sight, smell, taste, and touch*

PROPER 14

SUNDAY BETWEEN AUGUST 7 AND AUGUST 13 INCLUSIVE
LECTIONARY READINGS:
Genesis 37:1-4, 12-28
Psalm 105:1-6, 16-22, 45*b*

Romans 10:5-15
Matthew 14:22-33

TEXT: Matthew 14:22-33

PREPARATORY POSTURE: Go swimming.

EXPERIENCE: Invite the children to the front of the church at a different time in the service, an unexpected time. Talk with them about being on boats. Ask who has ridden in a boat. Discuss seasickness and other stories of boating. Be sure to mention how scary storms can sometimes be even when you are not on a boat.

Outfit the children with life jackets and take them on a pretend boat ride through stormy seas complete with flashing lights and sound effects. Suddenly, have a person walk toward them and invite them to step out of the boat, recalling Jesus' invitation to Peter. Lead each one safely out of the boat and back to shore.

SENSES: *Hearing, sight, and touch*

PROPER 15

SUNDAY BETWEEN AUGUST 14 AND AUGUST 20 INCLUSIVE
LECTIONARY READINGS:
Genesis 45:1-15
Psalm 133
Romans 11:1-2*a*, 29-32
Matthew 15:(10-20) 21-28

TEXT: Matthew 15:(10-20) 21-28

PREPARATORY POSTURE: Try to tie a piece of licorice around your tongue. Hold your tongue.

EXPERIENCE: We have heard of being tongue-tied, but have you ever tried to tie something onto your tongue? As children, we were told to hold our tongues. Ask the children what they are told when they say things they shouldn't. What happens to them? Are there still literalists who wash mouths out with soap? Discuss what children are told about what comes out of their mouths. Make tongue leashes or lassos out of licorice laces and attempt to tie down some tongues. It is almost impossible to tie licorice around the tongue. Since we can't tie our tongues down, we have to learn and practice what are the right and wrong things to say. The "back-to-school" context reinforces our need to control our tongues.

SENSES: *Hearing, touch, sight, taste, and smell*

PROPER 16

SUNDAY BETWEEN AUGUST 21 AND AUGUST 27 INCLUSIVE
LECTIONARY READINGS:
Exodus 1:8–2:10
Psalm 124
Romans 12:1-8
Matthew 16:13-20

TEXTS: Romans 12:1-8; Exodus 1:8–2:10

PREPARATORY POSTURE: Wade in a river or stream.

EXPERIENCE: Ask the children if they think they have any gifts. They will probably be as confused as adults are when responding to this question. Children know about buying gifts. Place a gift bow on each child's head, and suggest that rather than buy gifts for their parents or new teachers, they try to be gifts to their parents and teachers. Would someone want to receive them as a gift? Help the parents to remember what gifts these children were and are.

For small churches: Prepare a large box as a gift box and invite each child to hide in the box. Encourage their parents, guardians, or Sunday school teachers to open the box and receive the child as a gift.

Retell the story of the birth of Moses using the children as the reeds in the river and the river itself. They will love to say the names of the midwives, Shiphrah and Puah, who did what God wanted them to do. Let the children hide the baby in the basket. Then let them pass it over their heads to the daughter of the pharaoh, as if they were the flowing water of the Nile.

SENSES: *Hearing, sight, and touch*

PROPER 17

SUNDAY BETWEEN AUGUST 28 AND SEPTEMBER 3 INCLUSIVE
LECTIONARY READINGS:
Exodus 3:1-15
Psalm 105:1-6, 23-46, 45c
Romans 12:9-21
Matthew 16:21-28

TEXT: Matthew 16:21-28

PREPARATORY POSTURE: Go to an aerobics class or exercise to a video.

EXPERIENCE: Find someone in your church who is an aerobics instructor or a football coach and can lead the children in a calisthenics exercise. Ask that person to stand in front of the children and lead them through a short routine of movements. See if they can follow along without verbal instructions. Make it easy at first, but see to it that the activity becomes increasingly complex. Then try it with verbal instructions. Remind the children that following Jesus is not always easy, but we have the Bible and other people to help us as we try to carry our own crosses. Give each child a pocket-size cross to carry.

SENSES: *Hearing, sight, and touch*

PROPER 18

SUNDAY BETWEEN SEPTEMBER 4 AND SEPTEMBER 10 INCLUSIVE
LECTIONARY READINGS:
Exodus 12:1-14
Psalm 149 or Psalm 119:33-40
Romans 13:8-14
Matthew 18:15-20

TEXT: Matthew 18:15-20

PREPARATORY POSTURE: Seek a handshake of reconciliation with someone who may have sinned against you.

EXPERIENCE: Ask the children to shake hands with themselves. You can't really do it. Ask them to find someone in the congregation with whom to shake hands. Ask them, "Who is shaking hands with whom?" When we shake hands, we shake hands together. It takes both persons to shake hands. Remind the children that Jesus said, "For where two or three are gathered in my name, I am there among them." Ask the children to hold hands and form circles of two or three throughout the congregation. Make sure everyone is in a prayer circle. Ask everyone to look into one another's eyes. Do they sense God's presence with them? Close in prayer, encouraging those within the small circles to pray with and for one another. Tell the children, "Shake hands with your group members before you return to your seats, remembering God's presence. Two or three people can do some powerful things."

SENSES: *Hearing, sight, and touch*

PROPER 19

SUNDAY BETWEEN SEPTEMBER 11 AND
SEPTEMBER 17 INCLUSIVE
LECTIONARY READINGS:
Exodus 14:19-31
Exodus 15:1*b*-11, 20-21
Romans 14:1-12
Matthew 18:21-35

TEXT: Romans 14:1-12

PREPARATORY POSTURE: Read Dr. Seuss's *Green Eggs and Ham* to a child.

EXPERIENCE: Use Dr. Seuss's *Green Eggs and Ham* as a pattern for this children's sermon. At times, we are scared to try the new, but the eggs are still eggs, even if the green packaging is not what we are used to. The story also reminds us that persistence pays off.

Would you share Christ at your school? Would you share Christ at the swimming pool? Would you share him here or there? Would you share him anywhere?

I would not, could not at my school. I would not, could not at the pool, and so forth.

After he tries green eggs and ham, he is ready to eat them anywhere. Are we ready to share Christ anywhere?

Prepare some green eggs and ham, and offer the children a taste.

SENSES: *Hearing, sight, smell, taste, and touch*

PROPER 20

SUNDAY BETWEEN SEPTEMBER 18 AND SEPTEMBER 24 INCLUSIVE

LECTIONARY READINGS:
Exodus 16:2-15
Psalm 105:1-6, 37-45 or Psalm 145:1-8
Philippians 1:21-30
Matthew 20:1-16

TEXT: Matthew 20:1-16

PREPARATORY POSTURE: Visit a vineyard and pick some grapes.

EXPERIENCE: Begin by devising a job that each child in the church would be capable of doing. One idea would be to give each child a piece of paper and ask each one to get as many signatures as possible on that piece of paper. Everyone with signatures will get a reward, a coin if possible. Send out letters to a few children the week before with the paper, the instructions, and the promise of a reward for fulfilling the requirements. With a large group of children, send a few each day, the week before, making sure at least half the children get letters. Children love receiving mail! Give out a few more of the papers before Sunday school, and reserve a few papers to be given to children at the beginning of the children's sermon. While you are talking to the other children and reviewing their papers, have the latecomers get signatures from the congregation. Give everyone the same remuneration and talk about their feelings of fairness. God will be giving and generous to all, even when it doesn't seem fair to us!

SENSES: *Hearing, sight, and touch*

PROPER 21

SUNDAY BETWEEN SEPTEMBER 25 AND OCTOBER 1 INCLUSIVE

LECTIONARY READINGS:
Exodus 17:1-7
Psalm 78:1-4, 12-16
Philippians 2:1-13
Matthew 21:23-32

TEXT: Matthew 21:23-32

PREPARATORY POSTURE: Finish a job or project you have been avoiding, preferably a job that involves working outside.

EXPERIENCE: Children will love to hear and discuss the story of the two sons. Choose sets of three children to portray the story. Let as many groups as time allows reenact the story. Then separate the children into three groups: those who said they would work and didn't, those who said they wouldn't work and did, and the fathers/parents. Take a vote within each group to see what they think. Is it what we do or what we say that pleases God? Help the children decide. Is it both? Ask the children what they have done this week that would please God. With a small group of children, use adults to play the sons' roles and let the children experience the disappointment of being disobeyed. Remember that the sons are not asked to go into the field; they are *told* to go!

SENSES: *Hearing, sight, and touch*

PROPER 22

SUNDAY BETWEEN OCTOBER 2 AND OCTOBER 8 INCLUSIVE
LECTIONARY READINGS:
Exodus 20:1-4, 7-9, 12-20
Psalm 19
Philippians 3:4*b*-14
Matthew 21:33-46

TEXT: Exodus 20:1-4, 7-9, 12-20

PREPARATORY POSTURE: Attempt to write down the Ten Commandments from memory. Read Exodus 20 to check your list. Visit the local high school band director and/or theater props manager.

EXPERIENCE: For the risk taker: Create a scene in the sanctuary by loosing the sounds of thunder and visions of lightning upon the gathered children. A thunder sheet is a readily available theater prop, but a budding percussionist could also create the crashes of thunder. Flashing lights imitate lightning, while the sound of a trumpet is self-explanatory. A dry ice machine will provide the smoke from the mountain. Begin with a narrator speaking verse 1. Allow someone else to read the rest of the commandments. If children are afraid of the noises, calm them as Moses did. After this experience, discuss what they heard and saw.

A less risky alternative: Children are familiar with rules and know the kinds of things that displease their parents and teachers. Ask the children to make a list of things they think God would like us to do. Then add to the list things God does not like us to do. Help them compare those lists with the Ten Commandments. Give them a list of the Ten Commandments to discuss with their families at home. (Oriental Trading has pencils with the Ten Commandments written on the side.) For each of the next ten Sundays, give the children one commandment to learn by heart. This will take until the Sunday before Christmas and ties in rather well with the lectionary readings for each week.

For those celebrating World Communion Sunday: Make the connections between God's rules in the Ten Commandments and the repentance and forgiveness involved in Communion.

SENSES: *Sight, touch, smell, and hearing*

PROPER 23

SUNDAY BETWEEN OCTOBER 9 AND OCTOBER 15 INCLUSIVE
LECTIONARY READINGS:
Exodus 32:1-14
Psalm 106:1-6, 19-23

Philippians 4:1-9
Matthew 22:1-14

TEXT: Exodus 32:1-14

PREPARATORY POSTURE: Spend some quiet time on a
mountain or hill listening for God to speak to you.

EXPERIENCE: The Philippians text reminds us to rejoice
in the Lord always, not to rejoice in other gods, but the
story of the golden calf from Exodus 32:1-14 is the most
accessible for children this week. Ask someone who does
not usually lead the children's sermon to meet with the
children (for example, an Aaron when they are expecting a
Moses). Tell the children that the usual person said he or
she would be right back. Wait with the children. After a few
moments of waiting, take suggestions for what to do until
the leader comes back.

When the leader finally returns, retell the story from Exodus 32. Children will certainly relate to the impatience of
waiting for someone. Discuss all the things we do when
trying to pass the time while waiting. What are good things
to do while waiting? The people got tired of waiting for
Moses and decided to try worshiping another god. (From
the movies, we have come to see the golden calf as a huge
idol, but some scholars assert that it was probably a small
image like the little household gods that people carried
with them because it was made from the gathered jewelry
of the people.) What they did made God mad, but God
decided to forgive the people.

Be prepared to deal with the concept of God changing
God's mind. What would the children think of having their
jewelry melted down and made into the shape of a cow to
worship?

SENSES: *Hearing, sight, and touch*

PROPER 24

SUNDAY BETWEEN OCTOBER 16 AND OCTOBER 22 INCLUSIVE

LECTIONARY READINGS:
Exodus 33:12-23
Psalm 99
1 Thessalonians 1:1-10
Matthew 22:15-22

TEXT: Matthew 22:15-22

PREPARATORY POSTURE: Closely examine the contents of your purse or wallet.

EXPERIENCE: Most children have been tricked into saying or doing something that got them into trouble. Explain how the Pharisees tried to do the same thing to Jesus, getting him to say something for which they could arrest him. Give the children coins to look at and ask them what they see. Discuss phrases such as "In God We Trust" as well as the faces and symbols the children pick out. Ask, "Whose coins are these?" Jesus told the Pharisees to look at the picture on the coin to see whose money it was. Have they ever seen God's picture on a coin? So what should we give to God?

Children have trouble comprehending the rather abstract idea of worshiping money, but they can understand the absurdity of bowing down to money or singing hymns about money. Take a traditional children's song or hymn and substitute "money" for "God" to give them the idea of idolatry. For example, "This little dime of mine, I'm gonna let it shine," or "Money loves me! This I know." "O for a thousand dollars to sing." "Blessed assurance, money is mine."

This exercise will help the children to see the limits of money worship. Help them answer the question, "What do you have to give back to God?" Jesus reminds us to give to God what is God's.

SENSES: *Sight, touch, and hearing*

PROPER 25

SUNDAY BETWEEN OCTOBER 23 AND OCTOBER 29 INCLUSIVE

LECTIONARY READINGS:

Deuteronomy 34:1-12
Psalm 90:1-6, 13-17
1 Thessalonians 2:1-8
Matthew 22:34-46

TEXT: Deuteronomy 34:1-12

PREPARATORY POSTURE: Visit the oldest people in your community and talk with them about their spiritual journeys.

EXPERIENCE: Since this Sunday is usually the ending of daylight saving time, many people gain an extra hour. Bring some clocks for the children to turn back one hour. Ask them what they would like to do with an extra hour.

Plan a mission activity or suggest alternatives for children to use their extra hour productively so that they are filling time rather than killing time. Killing time in a sense dishonors God because we have taken on the name of Christ and should not be wasting time that could be used in God's name. Look at the life of Moses as an example. What could be accomplished if we all used that extra hour to awaken to the possibilities God has for us rather than catch up on our sleep? Use that time to get to know a saint! Invite the people to spend one hour this week with someone whom they don't know very well and get to know the person better.

All Saints Celebration: This will probably be the Sunday before All Saints Day, November 1. Use the children's moments as a time to honor those among you who have grown old gracefully. Define what a saint is for the children, acknowledging that we are all saints and sinners. Invite the children to identify and bring to the front of the church the adults whom they think of as saints. You may also want to remember with them the saints who have gone before us. Charge all the gathered saints to grow old gracefully, full of grace.

SENSES: *Hearing, sight, and touch*

PROPER 26

SUNDAY BETWEEN OCTOBER 30 AND NOVEMBER 5 INCLUSIVE
LECTIONARY READINGS:
Joshua 3:7-17
Psalm 107:1-7, 33-37
1 Thessalonians 2:9-13
Matthew 23:1-12

TEXT: Joshua 3:7-17

PREPARATORY POSTURE: Cross a river by boat, by bridge, or on foot.

EXPERIENCE: Just as we are to remember the Sabbath day and keep it holy, Joshua sets up a ritual to remember as we attempt to cross the rivers in our own lives. Set up a river with cords of blue rope. Have children at both ends of the rope make waves by rippling the ropes. A cedar chest might be introduced as a facsimile of the ark of the covenant. Select twelve people to carry the ark under the moving blue ropes. When they reach the first rope, lay the ropes on the floor. To symbolize the water in a single heap, use a large blue towel or sheet upstream from where the crossing is being made. Let all the children cross on either side of the ark. Expand the pericope to include the gathering of stones and place them where the ark once rested to help everyone remember how God delivered God's people into the promised land.

Adults will see the similarities to pallbearers carrying a casket across the river Jordan to new life. Tombstones are still used to help us remember our journeys.

SENSES: *Hearing, sight, and touch*

PROPER 27

SUNDAY BETWEEN NOVEMBER 6 AND NOVEMBER 12 INCLUSIVE
LECTIONARY READINGS:
Joshua 24:1-3*a*, 14-25
Psalm 78:1-7
1 Thessalonians 4:13-18
Matthew 25:1-13

TEXT: Matthew 25:1-13

PREPARATORY POSTURE: Check the batteries in your smoke detectors and flashlights. Examine your plan to cope with a power outage.

EXPERIENCE: Using flashlights and batteries, retell the story of the ten bridesmaids. Use five adults as the foolish maidens and five children as the wise maidens, all with dead batteries in their flashlights. Let the kids pack extra batteries just in case the bridegroom comes. Announce to them that the bridegroom has been delayed and they can rest until he comes. Then shout, "Look! Here is the bridegroom. Come out to meet him."

Encourage them to get up and try to turn on their flashlights. When none of the flashlights work, help the children put in their extra batteries while the adults beg for help. Send the adults out to buy batteries, and while they are gone, let a bridegroom in a tuxedo or your vision of the bridegroom arrive. Creative use of music can add to the drama of the bridegroom's entrance in the same way we create anticipation for the arrival of the bride in today's weddings.

When the adults come back, see that everyone has gone out a door to the wedding banquet. Send them to the door to ask, "Lord, lord, open to us." Whereupon they hear the bridegroom's reply, "Truly I tell you, I do not know you. Keep awake therefore, for you know neither the day nor the hour." Discuss how the adults and the children felt when the bridegroom came or when they missed him.

Veterans' Day will be celebrated on November 11. You may want to talk about the futility of long-range planning in times of war and crisis, when the best you can do is to be prepared.

SENSES: *Hearing, sight, and touch*

PROPER 28

SUNDAY BETWEEN NOVEMBER 13 AND NOVEMBER 19 INCLUSIVE
LECTIONARY READINGS:
Judges 4:1-7

Psalm 123 or Psalm 90:1-8 (9-11), 12
1 Thessalonians 5:1-11
Matthew 25:14-30

TEXT: Judges 4:1-7

PREPARATORY POSTURE: Visit a courtroom. Observe a trial.

EXPERIENCE: Invite a female judge from your area to play the part of Deborah this Sunday. Make sure that she is available after the service for the children to ask her questions about the role of a judge. This will allow the children to make a deeper connection with the judge and the story of Deborah.

The majority of heroes in the Bible are men, but here we have a story of two triumphant women, one who judges Israel and another who slays the opposing army's general. Borrow a palm tree from a local florist and station Deborah under it. Ask her to retell the story of Barak and Jael.

Jael's story is an exciting one and will captivate children's interest. The actions of Jael in the expanded pericope (to v. 22) can be contrasted with the admonition against murder from the Ten Commandments. Ask the children,"If you were the judge, what would you do about someone like Jael?" Perhaps that's how they can remember her name, they would want to throw her in Jael. Questions about capital punishment may arise; be prepared to help the judge answer these from within the context of your tradition. I will always remember the day when a third grader in pursuit of the God and Me Service Award asked, "If someone kills someone else in war, can they go to heaven?" Help the children struggle with the tension between the people who perceived God wanting them to kill their enemies with the teaching we give our children that killing is wrong. The discussion will be even more pertinent if this is the Sunday after Veteran's Day.

SENSES: *Sight, hearing, and touch*

PROPER 29

SUNDAY BETWEEN NOVEMBER 20 AND
NOVEMBER 26 INCLUSIVE

(Last Sunday After Pentecost or Christ the King)
LECTIONARY READINGS:
Ezekiel 34:11-16, 20-24
Psalm 100
Ephesians 1:15-23
Matthew 25:31-46

TEXT: Matthew 25:31-46

PREPARATORY POSTURE: Set an extra place at the table this week. Invite someone to share a meal with you.

EXPERIENCE: Around God's table there is always room for one more. Gather the children around the altar table if at all possible. Form a small circle with the altar in the center. Ask if there is room for one more. Add a few more people until the circle grows wider and wider. Invite everyone to join hands around the outside of the church after worship to show that the circle can always get bigger to include more and more people while keeping Christ at the center.

SENSES: *Touch, hearing, and sight*

NOTES ───────────────────────────────

1. Sam Matthews, "Learning Like Children," *Wesleyan Christian Advocate*, 9 September 1994, p. 5.

2. Carolyn C. Brown, *Gateways to Worship* (Nashville: Abingdon Press, 1989), p. 8.

3. William Armstong, *Five Minute Sermons to Children* (New York: The Methodist Book Concern, 1914), p. 6.

4. David Elkind, *The Hurried Child* (Reading, Mass.: Addison-Wesley, 1981), p. 97.

5. Leander Keck, *The Church Confident* (Nashville: Abingdon Press, 1993), p. 104.

6. Dick Murray, *Teaching the Bible to Adults and Youth* (Nashville: Abingdon Press, 1987), p. 57.

SCRIPTURE INDEX – YEAR A ___